The Labor Arbitration Career

Andrea L. Dooley

Contents

Foreword

To the labor and employment law advocate, labor arbitrators are a mysterious lot. Reminiscent of the Maybelline slogan, "Maybe she's born with it, Maybe it's Maybelline," the curious observer wonders how established arbitrators have developed a successful practice. Every arbitrator has their own story, but many of them hold their secrets—and their missteps—close to their chest.

At each stage of our careers, arbitrators have different considerations and decisions to make about how they want to develop their practice. By dividing the phases of an arbitrator's career into four parts, I will highlight these considerations and how they evolve to increase the arbitrator's success and satisfaction in their practice.

The four phases of an arbitrator's career include: starting, growing, maintaining, and ending. The distinctions among these phases are blurry; however, there are steps that you can take to ensure that your practice remains dynamic and sustainable during each phase. Arbitrators should find useful information and ideas in each section, regardless of how long they've been in practice.

In writing this book, I wanted to share the tips that I have received from more established arbitrators as my career has progressed and offer my thoughts regarding the long path of how my career has developed. Some folks, particularly other arbitrators, may wonder why I have undertaken this project. Because it's a solo practice, and the source of work is limited to labor grievances, many arbitrators prefer to keep the profession small. This is particularly true in areas of the country where there is low union density and it is difficult to maintain a business based on the cases available in their vicinity.

Nevertheless, I am fortunate to live in an area that has a higher union density than most parts of the country; there are many full-time arbitrators in Northern California. Moreover, I believe that the profession suffers from a lack of diversity and fresh perspectives. In order to better reflect the workforce, unions and employers, as well as their lawyers, must select arbitrators from a wider spectrum of backgrounds. In fact, the National Academy of Arbitrators considers Diversity, Equity, Inclusion, and Belonging (DEIB) to be "issues of critical significance, both in the broader world and in the Academy."[1]

In order to achieve this goal, the field requires more people who are interested in labor arbitration as a career. This book is an effort to demystify the career path for those people and provide guidance for individuals who have not found the support and mentorship of other arbitrators that is so vital to a successful career. Of course, I recognize that one book cannot fill that gap, but if I can spark the confidence of just one or two arbitrators who would not otherwise have found their way into this career, it will be worth it.

---

[1] 2021-23 NAA Diversity, Equity, Inclusion, and Belonging: A Strategic Plan, Special Committee Report to the Board of Governors. https://naarb.org/wp-content/uploads/2022/06/DEIB-Committee-Report-to-BOG_Final-3.22.pdf

Chapter One

Before You Quit Your Day Job

Are You Qualified?

One of the most common questions that I receive from people who are curious about becoming a labor arbitrator is, "What are the job qualifications?" People are surprised to learn that arbitrators do not have any kind of certification process, nor is there a licensing requirement to become an arbitrator. The only qualification is that you are acceptable to the parties who select you to hear their disputes. "Acceptable to the parties" means that you're able to get labor and management to agree to jointly select you. Essentially, both sides know enough about you to trust you to resolve their issue.

Granted, it feels like a circular problem: how can they trust you if they never take a chance to learn who you are? However, don't despair. This section will help you evaluate whether you are the kind of person who unions and employers would trust to resolve their disputes. Most successful arbitrators have some relevant experience, such as practicing labor law, acting as a labor mediator, or working as a union or human resources representative. If you have professional experience with labor disputes, labor law, or labor-management relations, you probably have the substantive knowledge to consider this career path.

For example, I received a labor law certificate in law school and worked for a teachers' union as a law clerk. I then practiced labor law for eight years and subsequently became a national coordinator for a large coalition of unions. Additionally, I oversaw health and safety in a large hospital system. The variety of those experiences provided me with the skillset necessary to tackle the substantive part of arbitration. One of my colleagues, on the other hand, was a union representative and federal mediator who then oversaw arbitration services for a government agency. He did not attend law school, but he quickly succeeded as an arbitrator because people trusted his skills as a neutral.

Start Planning Before You Leave Your Job

Many people become arbitrators or mediators while they are practicing in another field. Nurses, therapists, lawyers, contractors, and real estate agents can all call themselves a mediator or arbitrator in commercial or private arbitration without sacrificing the income they receive from their primary job. Labor arbitrators, on the other hand, cannot work in an advocacy role when they hear cases.

This is obviously a major barrier to entry in the labor arbitration field; however, there are good reasons for it. Because there are no licensing requirements or training qualifications to be a labor arbitrator, parties select neutrals based solely on their knowledge and experience in labor relations. The parties must believe with certainty that the neutral they select is just that—neutral. If someone who called themselves a neutral still worked for a union, an employer would justifiably be worried that the individual might be inclined to rule favorably for the union in every case, if only to preserve their livelihood working for a union. The reverse is obviously true as well. There are many people who argue that this rule should be applied to arbitrators in commercial practice and other neutral roles, but that's a bigger battle than what I want to tackle today.

Just because you can't work as an advocate while becoming a labor arbitrator doesn't mean that you can't start preparing for the job while working in a union or management job. There is so much that you can do to prepare yourself to launch an arbitration practice before you leave your old position. If you plan to become a labor arbitrator five to ten years from now, you can even find a career that will let you work while you arbitrate. I will discuss those options later in this chapter.

Training

Assuming that you would like to start your labor arbitration career in a shorter timeframe (e.g., a year or two), or you simply want to get a taste of what being an arbitrator is like, I recommend that you find a training program that will offer you a head start. The Federal Mediation and Conciliation Service ("FMCS") Institute offers a week-long training program called Becoming A Labor Arbitrator ("BALA") that is very thorough and does an excellent job teaching the basics of launching a new career.[2] In addition, if you complete the course, you receive credit toward the eligibility requirements to join their panel. Although the program is expensive—$2,700 at the time that I am writing this—it is worth the cost and time commitment if you are seriously considering the career change. BALA also connects new arbitrators to mentor arbitrators who are committed to supporting the fledgling careers of BALA graduates.

Build Your Network

Another proactive step to take before leaving your job is to determine who is in your network. Make sure that you have a personal list of your professional contacts on hand, especially if you will need to return your phone and laptop when you leave your job. Additionally, make sure that your membership in your professional organization is current. Local bar associations and human resources organizations are often looking for new ideas and volunteers. Start participating in or leading events that they sponsor.

---

[2] Federal Mediation and Conciliation Service, FMCS Institute, Becoming a Labor Arbitrator: https://www.fmcs.gov/fmcs-institute-registration/

Once you have your list of contacts, it's time to start reaching out to them. A career counselor once told me, "When you are looking for a new job, you have to do something every single day to get one. When you aren't looking for a job, you have to do something every week for your career—either the one you have, or the one you may someday want."[3]

This might sound overwhelming; however, there are many things that count as action. Creating lists, making phone calls, writing emails, scheduling appointments to meet or talk on the phone, writing "thank you" notes, and conducting research all count toward "doing something" when you are planning a career change.

When you reach out to people in your network, you must be mindful of how much you tell them. Other neutrals are a great place to start. Let them know that you are interested in becoming an arbitrator and ask them questions about the practice in your region. As a general rule, arbitrators won't speak to you if you have an active matter pending before them, so only approach people who are familiar with your work, but who you are unlikely to appear before in the coming months. Ask for their honest assessment of your chances of success, but don't be discouraged if they are not supportive. After all, you are proposing to become their competition. Think about their current reputation and ask how they became acceptable to parties to be selected. Ultimately, you probably have a different reputation and different expertise.

It can be difficult to call colleagues or clients to ask them about your prospects as an arbitrator; however, it makes sense to confide with one or two people who are familiar with you to find out if they believe that you have "judicial temperament" and general acceptability to the potential parties. If you are concerned that they will think you are "jumping ship" on your current position, you can note that this is a long-term plan and that you are just considering the options.

---

[3] https://tonilittlestone.com

Cataloging Your Skills

In addition to a list of contacts, create a list of your skills and experiences. Some of this entails resume building, but you should make a separate list of your so-called soft skills that will be good to have if you plan to become an arbitrator in solo practice. For example, do you work well alone? Are you well-organized? Are you patient? These are valuable skills to have if you plan to go out on your own. Making a list will also help you determine your knowledge gaps so that you can plan how to acquire necessary skills.

For reference, I also evaluated my gaps. In fact, I had considered becoming a labor arbitrator for approximately five years before I took the first steps to start my practice. My labor background was deeply grounded in my work for a firm that was strongly associated with unions, and I knew that I would need more experience and some distance from my reputation as a zealous advocate before I would become acceptable to the parties. This awareness helped me choose positions that offered me different experience before launching my arbitration practice.

After I left my law firm, I worked in a labor-management partnership where I learned a lot about mediation and dispute resolution. At the hospital, I learned about management and supervisory skills. What I enjoyed most about my firm was the friendships I had made and the camaraderie I felt. Thus, I was nervous about working alone. However, after eight more years of working with more difficult teams and supervising others, I felt ready to work by myself. In fact, I found that my personal friends were enough to sustain my need for social interaction.

Once I realized that I had filled in most of my gaps, I could see that my skills had grown in the interim five years. I had become a good writer and communicator, and I had fostered hundreds of good contacts in the labor-management community. I also had the confidence to successfully run a hearing. Recognizing all that I brought to the table gave me the encouragement I needed to start my practice.

It's also time to update your resume in a way that reflects your career evolution. When you become an arbitrator, you aren't applying for a single job. You will be providing your resume to new people constantly, and your resume should evolve as your business does. Updating your resume is another task that you can accomplish as you pursue your "do something every day" goal.

Write a Business Plan

Business plans come in all shapes and sizes. Business schools and the Small Business Administration offer classes on writing them. There are also entire books written about them. NOLO Press offers several low-cost options for starting a business that include sample business plans.[4] There's even a template in Microsoft Word for a business plan. On the other end of the spectrum, the founder of Southwest Airlines is said to have written his business plan on a cocktail napkin in an airport bar. However, for the purpose of starting an arbitration practice, it is sufficient to type up a document that includes the following:

- The type of work you plan to do
- Who your clients are and how you will find them (e.g., market and marketing)
- Where you will do the work (e.g., physical work location and target region to find clients)
- What start-up costs you will have (e.g., fixed costs, such as a computer and cell phone)
- What ongoing costs you anticipate (e.g., expenses, such as phone and internet bills)
- What you will charge (i.e., income) and how soon you can expect to increase it

---

[4] https://www.nolo.com/legal-encyclopedia/choosing-your-business

You may not know what you will put in each category just yet; however, this process will help you shape your task list as you prepare to take the leap. The next chapter should help you answer some of the questions that your business plan will raise.

Talk to Your Partner and Your Financial Advisor

If you are in a long-term relationship, hopefully, you've already floated this idea to your partner. If they are anything like my spouse, they might be a little reluctant to have you leave your salaried position for the prospect of a year or two of unpaid work. Accordingly, there are two major questions that you are going to need to answer: "How?" and "When?" The former can be answered with a business plan, as discussed. The latter should be answered after a consultation with a financial advisor.

I recommend that you seek out a certified financial planner (CFP), rather than an investment advisor with your bank.[5] CFPs are paid hourly by their clients; therefore, their financial incentives are aligned with your success. Investment advisors are paid either by their financial institution or on commission for selling financial products. Your CFP can help you and your partner determine how much you will need to save at your family's income level without your salary in order to start a business.

In my case, our financial planner told us in January 2014 how much we should save and then suggested that we review our finances in June with the intent of selecting a departure date from my job. In late February of that year, my boss told me that I would need to lay off most of my staff and do their work. After writing a business plan and talking about it in great depth with my spouse, I gave notice in mid-March to my company. This allowed them to use my salary to extend the date of planned layoffs and forced me to move quickly to hang my shingle. Ultimately, our financial plan helped us prepare for our needs, which we were able to cover before June.

---

[5] https://www.cfp.net/ Certified Financial Planner

Have Another Source of Income

My fifth year of arbitration practice was the first year that I made more money than I did in my previous full-time job. Thus, I'm very fortunate to have a spouse whose income is sufficient to cover our monthly costs. For most people, economic uncertainty is the reason why they delay launching an arbitration practice. This is unfortunate because it prevents otherwise qualified folks from becoming arbitrators. That being said, a high household income is not necessary to launch a practice; there are some professions that you can do while you start your arbitration practice. There is also some work that you can do in the labor arbitration field while you build your business. In the next chapter, I will discuss other work that you can do for arbitrators when you are starting out.

The most common source of income for new arbitrators is to start drawing their pension at retirement. Many people plan their arbitration career as a third act, knowing that their pension will cover their expenses. They might view arbitration as a part-time gig that keeps them in their field until they are "really" ready to retire. Those folks are sometimes surprised to find that their practice doesn't take off as quickly as they thought and feel that a real retirement might be more interesting. Others find success quickly, only to discover that they desire more time to do the things that they had always intended to do in retirement! Still, others find a happy balance and a fulfilling career as an arbitrator. Granted, retirees who arbitrate don't solve the problem that our profession has: finding newer arbitrators who bring fresh perspectives and long careers. Nevertheless, if it works for you, it's a good approach.

Another common route is through academics, particularly in areas of the country where there isn't enough labor arbitration practice to sustain numerous full-time arbitrators. Many law professors also arbitrate cases, and the reverse happens as well: arbitrators begin teaching. Law school isn't the only place in the academy where you find arbitrators; some teach business, economics, or industrial relations. Becoming an academic is probably more difficult than becoming an arbitrator, however, so unless you are willing to invest decades into your education and job search, the academy may not be the easiest route to take.

Many state and federal agencies have full-time neutral positions that can prepare you for an arbitration career. FMCS and state mediation agencies have full-time mediator positions. The National Labor Relations Board (NLRB) and Merit Service Protection Board (MSPB) have hearing officers, and many other federal agencies also have administrative law judge positions. Many state and local governments have neutral hearing officer roles, both in labor and employment, as well as other areas, such as housing, planning and building, education, and disability.

Several states and cities will even let you have outside employment as an arbitrator, assuming that you follow their rules regarding disclosure. Jointly administered Taft-Hartley funds are also a good place to find neutral work. You'll develop expertise in pension and healthcare issues, ERISA and securities law, and collective bargaining. Whether you are also able to work as an arbitrator will likely be determined by your employer, but it's worth exploring nonetheless.

Some arbitrators maintain a parallel career or law practice unrelated to labor relations while launching their arbitration career. In fact, one colleague had a thriving bankruptcy practice while arbitrating labor disputes.

Finally, you can always marry for money! Just kidding, of course. That said, a mutually agreeable approach to the financial aspects of a labor arbitration practice can be truly beneficial for a family. An arbitration practice allows scheduling flexibility so that you can attend field trips, take vacations, be a caregiver, and pursue your own interests, with the likelihood, if you succeed, of a very good, steady income as the practice grows.

Other Hurdles

In trying to identify all of the factors that someone should consider when trying to decide whether to become an arbitrator, I'm aware that there are practical realities that some people will face that I do not face as a straight white woman. Some of my colleagues have faced greater hurdles because of their race, sexual orientation, perceived disabilities, national origin, and other immutable characteristics.

These hurdles are often invisible to the new arbitrator. You have no idea whether and when you were excluded from a panel, or when you were placed on a panel to give the perception of diversity when the parties had no intention of selecting you. Some hurdles that are more visible include people assuming at the hearing that someone else is the arbitrator because they can't imagine "someone like you" could hold that position, or assuming that you know another person because you have the same immutable characteristic.

I'm not in a position to know the full scope of issues that might arise for someone who isn't me. Fortunately, we are at a moment in our profession when there are more arbitrators with more and different backgrounds who are willing to act as a mentor or colleague to new arbitrators.

It's also a moment, hopefully not fleeting, when unions and employers are actively seeking newer arbitrators with backgrounds more reflective of their own workforce. Several parties have started to include language in their CBAs requiring a minimum number of arbitrators from diverse backgrounds on their panels. For example, Philadelphia Police Department and their police officers' union agreed that 40% of their panels would have traditionally a present underrepresented arbitrators. The United States Postal Services and their unions are making similar commitments to diversify their panels. These efforts have been supported by the Ray Corollary Initiative, an organization founded by NAA Members Homer LaRue and Alan

Symonette to address barriers to entry for historically excluded arbitrators.[6]

Chapter Checklist

- ⚘ Complete a skills and gaps assessment.
- ⚘ Sign up for training.
- ⚘ Identify your contacts and start working on your professional connections.
- ⚘ Write a business plan.
- ⚘ Talk to your partner.
- ⚘ Talk to your financial advisor.

---

[6] https://www.raycorollaryinitiative.org/

Chapter Two

Starting an Arbitration Practice

Now that you have decided to start an arbitration practice, there are several logistical considerations that you will need to tackle first. If you've started a business or even a job before, most of these considerations won't be too surprising, but they still warrant your attention.

Since you have just started your business and don't have any income yet, you probably don't have an office. You still need a mailing address, though. I recommend that you get a mailbox at the post office or at a stand-alone mailing center such as UPS or Mailboxes Etc., among other options. Some people use their home address, but I would hazard against doing that. The day may come when you are sending very bad news to someone (e.g., upholding their dismissal) and they become angry enough that they want to talk to you about it. You don't want them to easily find your home address. It also appears more professional to have a business address. Although you will need your home address for certain things, such as opening a bank account, you should generally keep home separate from business in this regard. Mailboxes cost approximately $30 per month.

Speaking of bank accounts, set up your business checking and savings as soon as possible. Familiarize yourself with the documentation that you'll need. They may request a copy of a business license, which can be obtained from the city where you will be working. Most cities and counties have small business centers that can help you with a business license. Some municipalities will require that you have a business license, so now is a good time to get one. Then, return to the bank and set up that account. A separate credit card is also useful because you will be fronting the costs of some expenses, such as travel and reimbursable meals. I set a benchmark monthly amount to keep in my checking account. Before I had an office, I kept $2,000 in the account. I've since raised it to $2,500. This ensures that any costs I forgetfully incur will be covered.

Probably one of the most exciting aspects of starting your practice is getting business cards and letterhead. Aside from the basic information that you would expect on a business card, it is important to have your cards printed at a union printer, and request the union bug. The "union bug" is the logo for the union to which the print shop employees belong, and your union clients will look for it as soon as they receive your business card. Don't be worried that it will make you seem pro-union. Management knows that the unions expect to see it and, since they are unionized employers, they may be slightly pleased to see that you frequent unionized businesses. Letterhead is less common now since we generate most of our correspondence from the computer, but the same principles apply to stationery as they do to business cards. If you get it professionally printed, go to a union shop and ask for the union bug. Even if you don't get custom stationary, I recommend that you buy "thank you" cards to send to all of the people you are about to call for help as you launch this enterprise.

Arbitrators are very limited in how they can market themselves. The old-school arbitrators do not believe that we should advertise at all, and the degree to which you can advertise is limited by state bar rules, the National Academy of Arbitrators Rules of Professional Conduct, and good taste. Notwithstanding these concerns, I do recommend that you create a website. Nearly everyone who sees your name on a list of arbitrators will conduct an internet search for your name. With this in mind, I suggest that you conduct an internet search for your name right now. Is there anything in the search results that you would rather not have as the first thing that someone learns about you? Mine included writing that I had done in college, along with my father's genealogy website—not exactly information that I thought clients would need to have about me.

Having your own website ensures that the information they find is what you want them to know. Of course, it can be a simple website with your biography, resume, and contact information. Provide the link to your own website in your email signature and share the link widely. The more people who visit, the higher your website will show up in search engines. However, be careful about having people enter information in a contact form on your website. That's a good way to get hacked or spammed.

Make sure that the domain name of your website is easy to remember. It's becoming more common to tell someone your website address than it is to give them a business card. Your email address should also be easy to remember and professional. For example, people might not want to hire surferdude420@emaildotcom.

I have a blog on my website, and most importantly, I include my availability calendar as well. My availability calendar is a program that syncs with my personal online (i.e., Google) calendar, so when I block out a date in my personal calendar, it is blocked off on my website calendar. Many people have told me that they really appreciate being able to schedule a case with me quickly without numerous phone calls and unnecessary difficulty. If you are worried that your calendar will look too empty at first, remember that you can block off dates in your personal calendar and the person visiting your website will have no idea whether you are doing a hearing or eating lunch with a friend.

The next few items are ones that you should be aware of, but likely won't need right away: billing software, a library, and a court reporter. The library is the easiest. Until you've met a retiring arbitrator who wants you to take their entire library—and don't worry, you will—you can use the county law library. If you live in the city where you attended law school, you can probably use that law library as well. Libraries come in handy for conducting research, obviously, but the librarians are the true gem. If you come up with an idea for an article, they will be able to quickly help you locate the resources you need, from cases and articles to publications that might be interested in your work. I don't believe that an online legal research account is worth the cost. Lexis and Bloomberg, for example, are quite expensive.

If you have used Mint or Quicken before, you will probably be familiar with QuickBooks, which is a straightforward program for business accounting. It costs approximately $50 per month for a basic package and you can sync it with your bank accounts. A simpler and less expensive option is Harvest, which used to be $12 per month. However, it doesn't sync with your accounts, so you will end up having to do your financial stuff in a different program.

Often, the parties arrange their own court reporters. If you aren't familiar with any, ask other arbitrators about who they would recommend. Working with court reporters who are already familiar with labor arbitration is very useful because they don't need to be educated on the process or lingo, and they are used to the more freewheeling atmosphere of the arbitration hearing compared to a court hearing or deposition.

Government agencies have specific requirements to become listed on their panels or to get contracts for cases. The federal government requires that you have an account in the System for Award Management (SAM) to get a contract or be paid. Some arbitrators find SAM to be cumbersome and do not take federal cases in order to avoid it. Personally, I found it time-consuming to register, but not difficult to maintain. Part of your work will entail researching other requirements for government agencies to see how you can qualify for their work.

Track Down Starter Work

My earliest cases involved card check/recognition cases, writing and research work, and fact-finding cases. Fact-finding is an evidentiary process that occurs when parties have reached impasse and the hearing officer writes a non-binding recommendation for settlement. When I started, the California Public Employment Relations Board (CA PERB) paid only $100 per day to its appointed fact-finders, and at that daily rate, I was easily appointed because so few neutrals would work for such a low rate. Even $100 per day was more than I made sitting at home, and it was worth the experience. CA PERB is still looking for fact-finders because the statute requires that hearings be held within 30 days of appointment, and many experienced arbitrators cannot comply with such a short timeframe for scheduling.

My first case was with two parties whose representatives frequently used fact-finding. Although that case was not remunerative, they selected me for another two dozen cases over the next 18 months (at my regular per diem rate), which helped launch my practice. CA PERB now pays closer to the market rate, which is currently $1,200 per day.

There is often work available from other arbitrators that can generate income while you are waiting for your own cases. Several arbitrators hire ghostwriters, and several panels give mediation or low-fee cases to new arbitrators. In the past, arbitrators would hire people to act as their apprentices. The apprentice arbitrator would attend the hearing and assist with drafting the arbitrator's decisions or summarize the hearing transcripts. Before computers, apprentices likely did a lot of typing and re-typing of decisions, although perhaps secretaries did those tasks.

Unfortunately, the practice of hiring an apprentice has fallen out of favor; however, it's a great way to diversify the profession. In the 1970s and early 1980s, it was common for women to get their start apprenticing with established arbitrators. This allowed parties to become comfortable with the idea of a woman arbitrator. Women now make up a considerable share of the profession in many parts of the country.

Although I am not aware of any arbitrators offering a formal apprenticeship, I do know several who offer the parties a hearing officer model. In this model, a newer arbitrator conducts the hearing and the experienced arbitrator makes the decision. I don't know how often parties take up this offer when selecting an arbitrator, but some well-known arbitrators are booked a full year in advance, and this model may be the only way to achieve a swift resolution of a grievance from those arbitrators.

Recognizing that it can be difficult to ask an arbitrator if they use writers or are hiring, many arbitrators in need of assistance approach new arbitrators first. Take every opportunity to meet other arbitrators at bar association meetings, National Academy of Arbitrator (NAA) events, and Labor and Employment Relations Association (LERA) conferences.

Make Business Development Your Job

As an arbitrator, much of your time will be spent doing administrative work and business development, especially during the first couple of years. In the early days of my practice, I set a target to work every day at my arbitration business, and I gave myself credit toward that goal for everything I did. Get a business license, check your mail, put up a website, update LinkedIn, attend a bar association event, and write a "thank you" note. Everything counts. Applying to panels, writing letters to prospective parties, researching collective bargaining agreements (i.e., to find out how they pick arbitrators, when their panel might open, and how many of the arbitrators on their panel are still practicing), and helping organize conferences and seminars are all great ways to keep moving forward.

Decide How Much to Charge

Obviously, you can't coordinate your per diem rate with other arbitrators. Each year, however, FMCS publishes a survey that shows the range by state so that you can see how many people in your area charge at the top rate and low rate, as well as what the median is. The advice that I received from many people was to not underprice myself. In reality, parties do not avoid arbitrators because of their rates. Rather, they look at overall billing practices, as well as their ability to run a hearing and reach prompt, well-considered decisions. Someone whose per diem is low, but who charges for many full days for writing a decision, likely won't be selected again.

Research, Research, Research

When I say research, here's what I mean:

Identify the unionized industries in your region or state. Identify the big employers in these industries. Don't limit yourself to local businesses. UPS and the federal government are both major employer, in every state. Identify the unions and their counsel in those industries. Send your resume to everyone.

Find the public employment relations agency for your state. Many agencies have panels for arbitrators and hearing officers. Research how to get on those lists. The department of human resources in your state will have labor relations specialists who select arbitrators or know who makes those decisions. It's fine to call and ask about the process for selection in their office.

Look for professional organizations that are related to this work, including labor councils, HR groups, LERA, and state bar committees. Attend their public events with business cards in hand.

Look for the law firms and attorneys who represent unions and unionized employers. It is acceptable to send them your resume without violating rules against ex parte communication as long as they don't have a matter pending before you. If you know who the representative on the other side is, you should send them a copy as well.

Research collective bargaining agreements in your region. Most public sector CBAs are online, as are many private sector contracts. Look at the arbitration clause to see how they select arbitrators. Keep track of expiration dates; parties often refresh their arbitrator lists after or near the end of bargaining. If their existing list has openings because arbitrators on the list are no longer working, reach out mid contract via email to both parties and send them your resume.

Keep looking for new opportunities in other neutral roles. For example, some people get on the Financial Industry Regulatory Authority (FINRA) panel, which pays poorly, but is probably a great experience. Apply to the public employment boards of your state and other states to which you can easily travel, civil service commissions, and court ADR programs.

Local courts have mediation programs, and community organizations offer low-cost mediation services, and you may be able to obtain volunteer experience with them. Additionally, introduce yourself to many union and management representatives. Attend National Academy of Arbitrators conferences, state and local bar association meetings and conferences, and professional groups such as LERA and related non-profit fundraisers. Write short articles for blogs (e.g., your own or others), newsletters, and bar association publications.

Get Some Hobbies

It's crucial that you have other things to occupy your time while you are waiting for the work to roll in. One of my colleagues took up the piano, and another focused on stamp collecting. I decided to focus on exercise and writing (i.e., memoir and fiction). Additionally, I maintained a regular schedule that balanced my interests with my business development and stayed as busy as possible. Loneliness and depression are real side effects of starting a new career that has such a long on-ramp, and planning ahead to keep them at bay is critical to your mental health.

Call Yourself an Arbitrator

Regardless of whether you have any business on the horizon, start telling people that you are an arbitrator as soon as you hang your shingle. Do not say, "I'm trying to be an arbitrator." Instead, say, "I am an arbitrator." Say it a lot to yourself and to others. It is also important to have answers to the following questions. I've shared my answers as well, but you may want to say something different.

Are you busy? (Answer: "Not as busy as I'd like, but I'm doing a lot of business development and stuff is starting to come my way." OR "Busy enough, but I have a little room for more. Are you looking for an arbitrator?")

Are you pro-union or pro-management? (Answer: "I'm pro-collective bargaining. I think it's the best approach to labor relations.")

What's the best part about it? (Answer: "Making my own schedule. Getting to hear new stories all the time. Getting to help people resolve their differences. Being the decision-maker.")

Have a Long-Term Plan

After a really successful second year (i.e., due to those fact-finding cases), my third year was much quieter, and it remained pretty slow (with some exceptions) during my fourth year as well. That's when I started to panic. To be clear, I had cases; however, it just seemed like I should have been getting more. It was an arbitrary feeling. As a result, I decided that if business hadn't picked up by my fifth anniversary, I would reconsider the profession. I don't want to say that my business instantly picked up, but it increased incrementally every month, and after five-and-a-half years, I had slightly more work than I wanted. My cases are now scheduled as far out as seven months, and I don't anticipate another major decline because I am on quite a few panels. In retrospect, I wish that I had made a long-term plan earlier so that I wouldn't be worried about the ebbs and flows (or "feast and famine") of solo practice.

What to Wear

Male arbitrators have a pretty clear uniform for hearings: that good old suit and tie. An experienced arbitrator might occasionally be able to pull off a golf shirt or sweater with or without a sports coat, but you'd need to know the parties really well to pull that off.

Women arbitrators have a harder decision regarding what to wear at a hearing. There are many factors to consider, including personal style, regional norms, and weather. Professional women in Northern California can wear a more relaxed style than you would commonly see in Southern California, where women frequently wear suits and high heels. That doesn't mean that you need a separate outfit for each region, but you also don't want to be wildly out of step with what is considered professional in the area where you practice. Floral shirts are perfectly acceptable in Hawaii, for example. As you probably remember, many offices have air conditioning on high, while other rooms heat up very quickly with many people in them. Plan to wear layers.

Ultimately, the best rule is to wear clothes that make you feel confident and comfortable. Wear clothing that conveys the impression that you want people to have about you. For instance, I want to be viewed as judicious and collegial. I want to garner respect and not distract participants with anything that might give the impression that I am biased in any way. For example, I believe that flashy and expensive jewelry might signal to a working-class grievant that I am rich and thus "out of touch" with their concerns. I prefer to have my demeanor make more of a statement than my clothes.

The only gender-neutral admonition I have is that you should wear good shoes. By good shoes, I mean comfortable and in good shape. If you are conducting a site visit, or the hearing will be held at the worksite, wear appropriate shoes. Granted, "appropriate" depends on the worksite rules, of course, but in general, high heels, crocs, flip flops, sandals, and fabric shoes are a bad idea. Shoes should be leather or fake leather with a hard sole that protects the whole foot. It's fine to ask beforehand if there are any safety rules that you should be aware of before entering the facility.

Be Prepared for Success

As part of your long-term plan, consider what kind of workload you really want, how far you want to travel, and whether you are pricing yourself correctly in the market. When will you raise your rates? Should you find an office or an assistant? Do you want to try to publish or speak? When do you eventually want to retire, and are you saving for it? If you succeed beyond your wildest dreams, what will that look like, and how can you get there?.

Chapter Checklist

- ☀ Get a mailbox.
- ☀ Set up bank accounts.
- ☀ Get business cards.
- ☀ Conduct an internet search of your name.
- ☀ Consider getting a website.
- ☀ Register with SAM (www.sam.gov).
- ☀ Establish your rate.
- ☀ Figure out your billing process.
- ☀ Find some hobbies.

Chapter Three

Growing an Arbitration Practice

After several months, or even several years (I'm sorry to say), the new arbitrator will find that they are getting selected with greater frequency. As a result, it's time to shift to the arbitration work itself.

Develop Your Templates and Policies

The more that can be standardized, the better. Having template letters for accepting a selection, setting a hearing, sending a decision, and sending a bill will dramatically reduce the amount of busy work that the new arbitrator must do. Here are several examples of template letters I use.

Selection Letter

Thank you for selecting me as the arbitrator for the above-referenced matter. My availability for a hearing date can be found on my website. Please look at my calendar,

confer, and let me know what date you are requesting for the hearing.

If you would prefer that I provide you with suggested dates for the hearing, please provide me with a timeframe in which you would like the matter to be heard (e.g., within 30 days, during the month of June, etc.) and I will provide dates for your consideration.

During the COVID-19 pandemic, I encourage parties to consider using video conferencing to conduct hearings. I am able to host video conferences via Zoom, which allows for breakout rooms to caucus, and provide a pre-hearing conference to test the technology and discuss logistics with the parties. I would also note that video hearings are more cost-effective for the parties, as I do not incur travel expenses to conduct them. Note that I am also available to conduct in-person hearings at this time.

It is my preference to correspond via email without sending hard copies. If either party requires a hard copy of any correspondence, please let me know. I've attached my resume and rate schedule for your files. Thank you.

I look forward to working with you both.

Confirm Hearing Letter

This will confirm [DATE] as the hearing date in the above-referenced matter. Please advise me of the start time and location once you have agreed on them. Although I do not require a court reporter, I will assume that you will arrange for a court reporter if you need one. If you would like me to arrange for a court reporter, please let me know.

Please be aware that, upon completion of the decision, I destroy all exhibits and transcripts. If you'd like me to return these materials at the conclusion of the case, please let me know at the hearing and I will send them to the requesting party at their expense. Thank you.

Decision Letter

Attached please find the Decision and Award in the above-referenced matter. Please let me know if you need a hard copy by mail; I am happy to send it to you if needed.

You will each receive an invoice for half of the fees and expenses incurred in this matter by separate email. Again, please let me know if you need a hard copy by mail.

Finally, as you know, an arbitrator may not ethically offer an opinion for publication without the consent of the parties. Although I have not decided whether to offer this opinion for publication, please let me know if you object to me doing so. Thank you very much.

It was a pleasure working with both of you, and I hope to do so again soon.

In addition to letter templates, you can make template file cover sheets with information about each case, decision templates for each type of case you handle, subpoenas that the parties request, and policies you adopt. I recommend that you learn how to make fillable subpoenas in PDF format.

Arbitrators often adopt policies in response to problems that they've encountered or questions that they've received several times. Common policies include cancellation policies, file retention/destruction policies, subpoena policies, and video conference procedures, but other arbitrators create more extensive standing orders about issues such as pre-hearing conferences, witness preparation, court reporting, and closing briefs.

Decide How, and When, to Enforce Your Cancellation Policy

Cancellation: If the scheduled hearing is postponed or canceled with notice of less than 21 calendar days, the per diem rate for each day of hearing shall be charged if another cannot be set in its place.

The rising arbitrator must decide how and when to enforce every policy, but the cancellation policy is the one that causes the most heartburn. Some arbitrators are very strict and never waive their cancellation fees. Others waive them if they are able to fill the date with another hearing, or even if they are just glad that the day is free because they'd rather use it in another way. Other arbitrators will waive their cancellation fee if there is a true emergency (e.g., if a party representative has been hospitalized). One arbitrator counseled me, "Never discount your per diem rate. But one way to appreciate parties with whom you might have an ongoing relationship is to provide a professional courtesy to both of them by lowering or waiving your cancellation fee. Be explicit about it, sending an email that says, 'As a professional courtesy, I will waive the cancellation fee in this case.'" This will leave an impression.

Office and Staff

Many arbitrators are quite happy to carve out space in their home from which to work when they aren't at a hearing. At some point, however, the files and bankers boxes of exhibits begin to feel overwhelming, or the presence of others in the home makes it difficult to maintain the boundaries they need to get work done.

There are several options for working outside the home. The most obvious—and expensive—is to get an office in an office building. Some arbitrators find offices within other firms, usually a law firm whose attorneys would never appear before the arbitrator, such as tax attorneys or estate planners.

Some arbitrators get an office together to share costs and have colleagues at hand to discuss issues that arise. Some arbitrators join a co-working space, which is not optimal unless there's storage available. Bringing files back and forth every day isn't worth the hassle, although I did it early in my career when my neighbor was doing very loud construction.

During the pandemic, I found it helpful to have an office to conduct Zoom hearings that weren't interrupted by teenagers and the dog. Otherwise, it is mainly a place to store files. Fortunately, my office is very affordable and close to home.

Most arbitrators work completely alone, although some have an administrative assistant to help with scheduling, billing, and typing. I work with a legal secretary who types up my dictation and formats my decisions. She works for several arbitrators and is familiar with the common lingo of our field. I've never met her in person; all of our work is exchanged via email. It can be hard to find a treasure like this on your own. Ask other arbitrators if they can recommend anyone to help you out.

Where to Hold Hearings

Most of the time, parties will arrange the location for the hearing and the arbitrator will show up at the appointed time, assuming that they've gotten decent directions, which isn't always the case.

I know one arbitrator who would tell parties who refused to agree on a location, "If you haven't come to an agreement by tomorrow, I'll arrange a conference room at (the most expensive hotel in their city), order full tea service and meals, and bill you both." She reports that this usually works to settle the issue.

I am on several panels where both parties are from out of town and they've asked for my assistance in finding a location for our hearings. I use the conference center at my husband's law firm, which doesn't generally do labor and employment work. I recommend identifying a low-cost conference center that you can use. Many court reporting services, law libraries, and co-working places have them. My office has a conference room, but no place for the parties to caucus, so I don't offer to host at my office.

Later in this book, I have a chapter about video hearings and their pros and cons. One issue to be aware of is that sometimes the parties cannot agree on whether to have the hearing in person or via video conference. Arbitrators do have the authority to order a hearing if the parties cannot decide. See National Academy of Arbitrators Advisory Opinion No. 26.[7] It is far better to encourage the parties to find a middle ground to address concerns or to have a pre-hearing conference to sort out the reasons for the parties' positions. Sometimes, concerns can be addressed easily; other times, the reality of COVID-19 in that particular area governs. For example, parties who intend at the time of scheduling to meet in person might realize that transmission rates are unacceptably high when the date of the hearing arrives.

---

[7] https://naarb.org/advisory-opinions/

Getting Paid

One of the more frustrating aspects of every arbitrator's job is collecting unpaid invoices. There are several ways to increase the chances that you'll have money coming in the door.

Make sure that you have a deadline for payment. Some arbitrators note, "Bill due upon receipt," on their bill, while others state, "Due within 30 days of receipt." Choose a window that you are comfortable with enforcing. Decide whether you intend to charge interest or a late fee on past-due bills. For about one year, I charged interest after 30 days. However, I stopped charging interest when I decided that it was too hard to collect and the amount due was confusing to administer. Billing software can calculate the interest on the unpaid amount, but there is some work involved when interest has accrued, but the delinquent party has paid the underlying bill. It seems like a hassle to send a second bill for the unpaid interest. It might be easier if you have someone who assists with billing, but if you are solo, figure out what's manageable for you.

A system for following up on unpaid bills is critical. Mark a day in your calendar each month when you will review unpaid invoices and send reminders. I advise against using the automatic reminders that can be sent by your billing system. They look like spam, and people tend to ignore them when they come too often.

If an invoice is older than 90 days, reach out directly to the advocate. Arbitrators are split on whether you need to let the other party know as well. Some arbitrators believe that you should have no ex parte contact, even if the matter is over. Others believe that if the matter is completely over, you don't have to copy the other party. They may feel as though it would cause embarrassment for the delinquent party when there may have been an oversight. If they are non-responsive to a direct request for payment, include the other side. Technically, both parties hired you jointly, meaning that they are both responsible for the whole bill. Asking the other side to get involved is a good way to get paid, either because of the embarrassment it triggers or because the other party will follow up on your behalf to avoid embarrassment to themselves in your eyes. Some arbitrators include language in their rate schedule about joint and several liability for their costs so that they can recover from either party if one party isn't paying their share.

Consider interim billing. Some arbitrators send a bill after the hearing and another bill after the decision. If you plan to do this, it's wise to disclose it in your rate schedule, just as you should disclose other billing policies. Other arbitrators prefer to wait until the matter is finished before billing the entire case. I take the middle road: I reserve the right to interim bill in my rate schedule, but only do so when the case drags on a long time, I've incurred significant expenses, or the matter will be expensive. I don't do it in every case because I complete my own bookkeeping and prefer not to double the number of bills I send out. I am also established enough that my income is fairly regular at this point.

Be aware that some organizations, particularly large companies and government agencies, are hard to collect from. They have complex accounting systems that are intended to prevent fraud, waste, and abuse; however, these are barriers to payment. Do not be shy when it comes to asking about the payment process ahead of time. Some arbitrators indicate in their rate schedule that they will charge for time spent having to comply with burdensome procurement requirements.

It also helps to find out who within an organization is best able to help you. Often, that's a very helpful person in accounts payable who will make sure that your bill gets paid if you send it to their attention. As always, being kind to support staff is good karma and will literally pay dividends. If you were appointed from a panel, enlist someone at the appointing agency to help. AAA and FMCS are both willing to become involved, if necessary.

Arbitrators in other practice areas often request prepayment of some fees. I haven't had an occasion to require prepayment, but my rate schedule does indicate that individual employees who are not represented by a union may be asked to make a deposit equal to the number of hearing days they schedule. An individual who loses their case seems less likely to pay and would be harder to collect from than an institutional client.

If none of that works, you might need to file a small claims suit to recover your money. I know some arbitrators who have done this. It seems like more trouble than it's worth to me, and the result will be that they won't hire you again and may speak ill of you to others. That's a calculation that you'll need to make.

The oldest bill that I ever had was approximately 16 months old. I was about to write it off when I learned that the union's new business manager was someone who I had once worked with. I reached out and he promptly got it resolved. In another situation, a law firm selected me for a scofflaw client of theirs. I told them that I'd only accept the appointment if the client paid their old invoices. There were embarrassed by the lapse and ensured that my old bills were paid. The law firm also provided me the name of the client's bookkeeper who has consistently paid the bill on time since.

Don't be shy about collecting your bills. Everyone understands that this is your business and expects that you will be as firm and professional in your collection efforts as you are in your decisions.

Get Your Ideas Out There

With just a few cases under your belt, you can start to share your ideas with the larger labor relations community. Ask parties if you can submit your decisions for publication and if they consent, do it. In a later chapter, I discuss the value of publishing your decisions. Write short articles for online and print journals. Offer to volunteer at conferences recruiting speakers and you will quickly find yourself on a panel to discuss a topic that you are confident you have mastered.

Network, Network, Network

For the introverted arbitrator, networking is one of the worst aspects of the job. The shy arbitrator is ready to surrender the task as soon as they've made it onto some panels. Unfortunately, the work doesn't stop at a few selections. It's important to attend conferences, dinners, and bar association events to introduce yourself to new people and remind others that you are still out there. Since you cannot have *ex parte* discussions with any party who has a pending case, these are good opportunities to introduce yourself and your style to people who make selections. Make sure that you have your business card on you at all times. I was once in a cell phone store buying a new charger and the young man helping me asked what I do for a living. I hedged a little, assuming that he wouldn't know what a labor arbitrator was; however, it just so happened that he was the chief steward for his union and a member of their bargaining committee. He asked for my card to share when they built their panel of arbitrators in the upcoming contract.

Find Your People

As previously mentioned, being an arbitrator is a lonely job at times, even when your practice has found its footing. That's why it's important to connect with your colleagues on a regular basis. It's useful to meet with other people who are roughly at the same stages of their careers to hear how they're handling similar problems or to learn about new opportunities. It might be intimidating at first because it may sound like their practice is "better" than yours, but you'll quickly learn that every arbitrator, even the most established ones, see their practice experience lean times. In addition to your peers, it's important to cultivate relationships with more experienced arbitrators who can act as mentors. Mentoring arbitrators, or in the case of many areas of the country, rising arbitrator salons hosted by established arbitrators, are an excellent way to learn and get new ideas.

Several regions of the National Academy of Arbitrators convene meetings that include non-member arbitrators by hosting "salons" to which new arbitrators may be invited. Typically, the salons are looking for newer arbitrators who intend to make arbitration their careers rather than post-retirement pastimes. The salons aim to ensure a diverse group of individuals to increase professional participation by historically excluded people.

Many mentor arbitrators will suggest to parties the name of rising arbitrators with whom they discussed cases. If they have a personal connection with you, they are more confident that their recommendation will be well-received and that the new arbitrator will impress the parties.

Preparing to Join the Academy

Not every labor arbitrator decides to join the National Academy of Arbitrators. However, the benefits of doing so are many. There are several national collective bargaining agreements that require membership in order to be considered for cases. All of the professional sports leagues require it, for example, as do many of the airlines. In addition to the camaraderie of other professional arbitrators and extensive continuing education opportunities, the Academy offers opinions on ethical issues and helps arbitrators with legal troubles. They give you a nice lapel pin when you join, too.

If you are considering joining, I recommend that you begin preparing as of your first decision. You will need to submit the cover page and last page/signature page of 60 decisions in order to be considered, and you might as well keep track from the very beginning. In fact, I maintained a folder called NAA Application where I kept a copy of every decision I wrote and an Excel spreadsheet that included the date, party names, type of hearing, and whether the decision was final and binding. When it came time to apply to the NAA, I had most of my materials prepared, making the application less difficult than it would have been without my planning.

Be Mindful of Ex Parte Communications

At the beginning of the arbitrator's career, the phone doesn't ring and the emails are all spam. Thus, when parties begin reaching out, or you run into party representatives who've selected you at non-hearing events, it can be tempting to get chatty. Being an arbitrator is a lonely job, and it's easy to let down your guard when it comes to this important ethical consideration. However, the rule is very clear: you can have individual conversations about scheduling issues, but otherwise, do not speak to one party without the other, and do not email or communicate in any other way with only one party. If one party attempts to steer an otherwise acceptable conversation towards a substantive topic, it's important to be explicit that you cannot discuss the topic.

The biggest pitfall is the downtime in the hearing room. Some arbitrators will exit the room if only one party is present. Others will bury their head in their phone, book, or laptop, and ignore the other people in the room. If there's a court reporter, it's easy to direct all of your attention to that person. Other arbitrators believe that topics such as the weather or local sports team are fair game when they are unrelated to the case and it's easy to include the other party in discussion when they return. An arbitrator's level of friendliness in a hearing is a judgment call for each arbitrator. In some cases, chit-chat will give the impression of favoritism. In other cases, chit-chat is useful for putting an anxious witness at ease in an uncomfortable forum. There are no cases, however, when it is acceptable to mention or discuss any aspect of the case without both parties present.

Sometimes, one party will notify you of your selection without including the other side. The best practice is to ask for the contact information of the other side before proceeding with other administrative matters. If a party reaches out during a case, remind them to include the opposing party, and copy the other party as well.

Don't Forget Disclosures

As with *ex parte* discussions, it is very important to make disclosures for each case. On one level, this might mean supplying your resume each time you are selected for a case, even if you know that the party has it. In labor arbitration, if you worked for a law firm or government agency, it isn't necessary to disclose every single client or case that the firm or agency had. However, if you directly represented or participated in a case involving one of the parties, it's important to disclose that. Usually, the parties are aware of it, and sometimes, they've selected you for your expertise in that area. Even if you believe that they know, still disclose both party names and individual names with whom you worked in a previous position. In labor only, you do not need to disclose to one party if you've been selected by the other party for a previous arbitration case, but you must do so in every other area of arbitration, including employment cases.

On rare occasions, you will learn during a hearing that you know a witness or party representative who wasn't previously disclosed. Stop the hearing and make the disclosure. I've done this several times and it has not made any difference to the parties, who have always wanted to proceed. For example, in one case, the HR director for the employer was a parent at my child's school. I only knew her as so-and-so's mom, but I disclosed the connection when I learned that she held that position. Disclosures increase the parties' confidence in your honesty and neutrality. If they should elect to proceed with another arbitrator, you have at least put yourself above suspicion in an ethical dilemma.

Chapter Checklist

- ☀ Make templates for all documents or languages that you will regularly use.
- ☀ Write policies regarding cancellations, video hearings, subpoenas, and any other issues that you anticipate encountering more than once.
- ☀ Keep your resume current.
- ☀ Keep a record of your decisions.

Chapter Four

Maintaining an Arbitration Practice

Around the time that you have your first negative experience, you may begin to get cold feet about this career you've chosen. For me, a party representative who had selected me quite a few times sent me an email saying that he would, "NEVER EVER" select me again. I had just raised my per diem rate, and suddenly it seemed as though the selection letters had come to a halt. It may have been a coincidence, but it worried me. As a result, I gave myself an ultimatum: if my arbitration practice hasn't taken off completely in one year—by my fifth anniversary—I would look for something else.

In the ensuing months, I became so busy that I forgot to take stock. Eighteen months later, I remembered my promise, chuckled at how I had blown past my anniversary, and started to think about the next stage of my career: maintaining an arbitration practice.

Take Stock

It's important to re-evaluate your business plan at least every five years. Taking stock means keeping track of where you get your cases, whether the processes you set up in your growing stage are still serving you, and whether you are working at a sustainable pace. I know arbitrators who reached this stage and realized that they had intended for this to be their retirement activity, not a full-time job. Others realized that labor arbitration alone wasn't paying the bills (i.e., financially or intellectually) and decided to branch out into other areas. Have you outgrown your office or workspace? Have you outgrown the suits that you bought at the beginning of your practice? Figure out what you want to keep, what you want to change, and how you will adjust your practice to make it even more of your dream job.

In particular, it's a good idea to evaluate two major areas that impact your quality of life. The first is calendar control. Even the most successful arbitrators worry that their next case may be their last, making it difficult to turn down work or schedule cases in a reasonable way. As a result, some months are completely overflowing with work. Many arbitrators are gambling that approximately 40 percent of their cases will be canceled or rescheduled, but when they don't, it's exhausting.

When this begins to occur, it's important to build in time for the rest of your life. For example, don't schedule hearings on Mondays or Fridays. One way that I keep my calendar somewhat open is to reserve hearing dates for a panel that rarely uses the dates I provide. They want six days per month set aside for their hearings! I give them four, knowing that they'll probably just use one. When they invariably cancel, I designate them as "writing days" and leave the date blocked on my calendar.

The other area to consider is whether you are charging a reasonable rate or whether it might be time to increase the per diem you charge. I raise my rates every three or four years. Unlike billing in private practice, I don't believe that unions and small businesses can absorb big year-over-year increases. At the same time, they understand very well that cost-of-living increases are warranted. You know your region best and what per diem rate they can bear.

Once you are in the "maintenance phase" of your career, it's also time to consider what you can give back to the profession. Mentoring other arbitrators is a rewarding way to ensure that the profession is diverse and growing. There are numerous volunteer opportunities with the NAA, law schools, and bar associations.

One last area to take stock of is your business reputation. As arbitrators, our highest value is our neutrality and integrity. You need to maintain acceptability to the parties—even the ones who haven't selected you yet. Evaluate whether you are giving the parties what they want: fair, concise, well-reasoned, and prompt awards.

Nail Down Your Writing Process

At this point, you will hopefully be getting enough cases that you will need to balance your writing time with your hearing time in a thoughtful manner. Some arbitrators can juggle multiple decisions at once while others work on one until it's done and then pick up the next. When you become busy enough, juggling will be unavoidable.

Here's one approach: at the end of the hearing day, record all of your thoughts, preliminary impressions, and relevant details such as issues, contract provisions, and witness summaries. If you have an assistant, you should dictate this information. It takes approximately 10 minutes to say the same thing that takes an hour or more to type out. Most word-processing programs have built-in dictation at this point. If you don't have an assistant or feel comfortable dictating, you should record this information in typed notes, or take detailed notes in the framework of a decision template during the hearing. Once you receive closing briefs, read them to refresh your memory, and then look at the transcript and documents while referring to your existing notes so that you can add details and citations. I always regret it when I have not prepared parts of the decision before I get the closing briefs. It's so much more time-consuming to write a decision six weeks (or more) after the hearing.

Here are several other thoughts about writing:
1. Do not make the perfect the enemy of the good. As stated previously, parties want fair, concise, well-reasoned, and prompt awards. They don't need Pulitzer Prize-winning decisions; rather, they need Dear Abby. Do your best and get it out the door.
2. Remember your audience. Most arbitrators say that they write their decision for the losing party. The decision should make it clear what facts and arguments were considered and how the

arbitrator reached their decision. I assume that this is a decision that will be read by frontline workers and human resource employees who were not familiar with the original grievance. I am writing for those readers—not the lawyers who argued the case.

3. Even if the contract doesn't require a decision 30 days after closing arguments, impose that deadline on yourself. The parties will appreciate it, and it will help you space out your writing days without letting anything become lost. If they ask for an extension on their briefs, you can give yourself an extension on the decision, but only if you need it. Treat the award like a hot potato and get it out of your hands. Then bill them!

Wrangling the Representatives

The level of tension and animosity in labor-management relations runs the gamut from collegial to vituperative. While many representatives complete their cases with professional efficiency, others insist on turning everything into a battle royale. Sometimes, you can tell this from nasty email exchanges about scheduling, and other times, you don't find out that they or their clients hate each other until everyone is in the hearing room. Either way, managing the feuds is part of the job.

One way to minimize the problem is to have a case management approach that is disclosed to the parties ahead of time. Some arbitrators have a case management order that sets forth "the rules," such as timelines, document and witness disclosures, or a pre-hearing telephone conference to reach an agreement on the issues. I've heard some attorneys grumble about this, particularly the ones who don't spend much time preparing before the hearing. However, as I tell my kids, "Your lack of preparation is not my emergency." If your case management process is known ahead of time, then those folks won't select you and you won't have to deal with their lack of preparation.

A case management order won't eliminate disagreement, of course. Sometimes, the hostility between parties is so great that it explodes during the hearing. There are some attorneys and representatives who use emotion as a performance tool. They will shout, curse, and threaten the other side. As the umpire, it's the arbitrator's job to manage the situation. De-escalation has several steps.

1. Ask the representatives to address their arguments to you, not to the other side. One arbitrator I know tells the parties, "If you make your objections to the other side, I'll let them rule on them." That can serve to re-direct the person who didn't realize that they were being argumentative.

2. Call for a short break. This can be done with or without calling attention to the purpose of the break.

3. Call the representatives out into the hallway and tell them the next steps in your de-escalation plan. In front of both of them, say, "The arguing needs to stop. If it happens again, I'll say something in front of your clients. If it happens a third time, I will adjourn the hearing for the day and we can resume when you are prepared. Your clients will have to pay for another day of hearing in order to complete this matter. Do you understand?"

4. If it happens again in the hearing room, say, "As I warned counsel, the arguing needs to stop so that we can make a clear record of the evidence. This is the last warning. If it happens again, I will adjourn the hearing for the day and we can resume on another day when everyone has cooled off. I will, of course, be charging for the additional day of hearing."

5. After that, if they argue or yell again, close your laptop, pack your bag, and leave. Do not give any other notice besides, "I will contact you in a few days about rescheduling this matter. I hope you will use that time to defuse the emotions around this case." Then go enjoy the rest of your day.

Get Help

Hopefully, you are busy enough that you can find clerical support. Of course, you don't have to hire your own legal secretary. Ask other arbitrators if they work with anyone who would like more work, or place a request with other practitioners to see if they'd like to hire someone with you. Clerical help with regard to formatting, transcribing notes, and sending form letters makes a huge difference. Some arbitrators have full caseload managers; others have schedulers. Figure out what you dislike the most about your practice and pay someone else to do it.

If you are busy enough, it may be time to consider hiring someone to help with drafting your decisions. Arbitrators are ethically bound to make the decision themselves; however, that doesn't mean that you can't get assistance from someone to draft the facts in your decision, do legal research, or write a first draft of your opinion, as long as the opinion is your decision. This can serve as great experience for a new arbitrator, but you can also hire a law clerk, the same way that a federal judge would.

If you haven't already, it's also time to find software that can help with billing, such as Quicken or Harvest. Labor arbitrators have a particularly way of splitting the bill between the parties that can be difficult to format in these programs, but it's worth learning. Better yet, hire a bookkeeper to set it up for you.

If you don't already have insurance, it's long past time to get some. In fact, many municipalities and bar associations require proof of insurance. There's professional liability insurance, business liability (i.e., general policy) insurance, car insurance, home insurance, and an umbrella policy. In the next section, I will discuss how to figure out what you need. I've included resources in the appendix as well.

Building Out Your Practice

There are many different directions in which you can take your career. Some people find that they prefer mediating disputes. Some neutrals expand into other arbitration practice areas, such as employment or commercial disputes. Be aware that other practice areas have different ethical requirements and expect other qualifications.

Although I prefer to stick with labor arbitration, I have expanded my practice through writing articles and practice guides, and by teaching Labor Arbitration at the University of California Berkeley Law School. Look for other opportunities through colleagues and professional organizations.

In my experience, the cases themselves have become more challenging as my career has progressed. My first impression was that unions were no longer taking simple matters to arbitration, or that employers were settling cases more readily. When I mentioned this to a colleague, however, he noted that simpler cases go to newer arbitrators, and that I was now being selected for the trickier issues. Building out your practice includes expanding the number and kinds of issues with which you are familiar. This means continuing to research legal issues and discussing them with your colleagues. The network of arbitrators you find will be one of the most valuable resources on which you can rely for talking through complex matters.

Get Even More Help

It is imperative that you retain other professionals to assist you in each stage of your career. Again, I highly recommend that you meet with a CFP to establish your financial goals, especially if you did not do so when you started your practice. In addition to helping you think about retirement, they can tell you what kind of insurance you need, what kind of tax planning and charitable giving you should consider, and how much of your income is "fun money." A CFP is paid by the hour and does not work for a particular bank, brokerage firm, or insurance company. This ensures that they have your interests in mind—not a sales target. Meet with a CFP for two hours every couple of years to keep your finances tuned up.

You also need to meet with an estate planner. The CFP will help you determine what to do with your money while you are alive, and an estate and trust lawyer will help you determine what to do with it when you're dead. Many people avoid this and leave their family in the position of spending a lot of time in probate court, having to make difficult decisions regarding your medical care, or scrambling to figure out what resources you left your family. This is not a "do it once and forget it" task, but it's close. You should revisit your estate plan every 5-10 years, depending on how many life changes you've made. For example, when my grandparents died, their will specified, "Custody of Joey and Michael to their uncle Frank." By the time of my grandmother's passing, Frank had been deceased for more than 20 years. "Joey and Michael" were 63 and 60, respectively. The estate was a mess. Keep your estate plan reasonably current.

In Case of Emergency, Break Glass

Crises happen. In addition to an earthquake kit and a "go bag," you need a plan for what happens to your practice if a crisis occurs. If you become incapacitated or worse, who knows how to contact the parties who have selected you? Who will help finish your awards or help the parties select a new arbitrator? Labor arbitrators would be well-served by a buddy system. If something goes wrong, your spouse or next-of-kin should know who to call to help manage putting a practice on hold or winding it down. Your spouse or next-of-kin should also know the password to your computer and have a key to your office and files.

Chapter Checklist

- Review your business plan.
- Review your billing rates and policies.
- Improve your writing skills or get an assistant to help with writing.
- Review your estate plan and create an emergency plan.

Chapter Five

Technology and Ethics

Alito and Sotomayor suggested that the Supreme Court may be too formal, isolated and technologically backward. Sotomayor cited two reasons for the court's reluctance to use technology. One was tradition. "The other," she said of some of her colleagues, "is they don't know how.8

M ost neutrals now use email; however, it was less than a decade ago that most people believed that email was too informal, and was possibly inappropriate for communicating about even basic issues such as setting meeting or hearing dates. Most people still faxed hard copies of these communications to one another, believing that fax confirmation was the best record for showing that there was no ex parte communication or that every party had notice of the relevant information. However, with the rise of e-filing in state and federal courts and the acceptance of electronic service, most attorneys have shifted to the current mindset, where email is widely viewed as the best and easiest way to ensure that all parties are communicated with simultaneously, and that the record is kept digitally, rather than on that old fading fax paper.

There are pitfalls and opportunities for neutrals in this technological framework. Although the ethical issues that email and social media create are not new, the availability of the technology

---

[8] "The Supreme Court Justices Return to Yale," Adam Liptak, New York Times, October 25, 2014.

multiplies the opportunities for ethical issues to arise. The informality of social media can create conflicts of interests, magnify inappropriate conduct, and provide additional opportunities for ex parte communications and disclosure issues.

Ex Parte Communications

Social media provides multiple platforms for people to communicate with one another. The informal nature of this communication may lead some to feel as though these communications are private and exempt from the usual rules of ex parte communications. This increases the likelihood that a neutral might have ex parte communications with a party. In 2010, Georgia Superior Court Judge Ernest "Bucky" Woods retired after emails surfaced showing that he had initiated a Facebook relationship with a defendant, who later tried to borrow money from the judge.[9] Judge Woods told the Fulton Country Daily Report that he retired because, "I just got tired of living under a microscope." While contacting a defendant has never been permissible, the email trail created by Facebook undoubtedly hastened Judge Woods' exit from the bench. In 2013, Texas State District Judge Elizabeth E. Coker resigned following complaints that she had texted the prosecutor during a criminal case, where the judge recommended questions that the prosecutor should ask during the trial.[10]

A higher-profile example of a judge being forced to resign due to ex parte communications occurred when Randall R. Rader, who had served as chief judge of the U.S. Court of Appeals for the Federal Circuit in Washington, retired after an email he sent an advocate surfaced. Rader sent Edward Reines, a lawyer at Weill Gotshal & Manges LLP, an email praising Reines' skills in a case before Judge Rader and invited Reines to share the email with clients. A friendship

---

[9]*www.abajournal.com/news/article/ga/_judge_resigns_after_questions_raise d_about_facebook_contacts/*

[10] http://www.chron.com/news/houston-texas/houston/article/District-judge-resigns-in-texting-case-4913627.php

that may have remained private in the past was easily rebroadcast, and discovered, via email blast.[11]

Although these are high-profile examples of ex parte communications that should be avoided, there are pitfalls even in the day-to-day use of email and social media. When communicating about routine matters, neutrals should ensure that all party representatives are included in reply emails and copy excluded parties to prevent accusations of ex parte communication. For example, if one party requests a continuance without copying the other party, it is appropriate for the neutral to reply to the requesting party, with a copy to the other party, stating that you will consider the request after hearing from the other party. While disclosure requirements (discussed below) are clear for existing relationships, neutrals should avoid having social contact of any kind with parties who currently or recently appeared before them.

Texting most resembles a telephone call and should not be used by neutrals to communicate with parties, except in limited circumstances. Texting should be used when the parties are not available by telephone, and all parties should be included in every text. A limited example might be a text to tell the parties that the neutral's train is delayed and that she expects to arrive 10 minutes late. Substantive communications should not be conducted by text.

Inappropriate Materials

In general, neutrals should be very cautious about email content—even personal emails intended solely for family members. It has become routine for public figures to be embarrassed by the disclosure of email content that does not reflect well on their character. Pennsylvania Supreme Court Justice Seamus McCaffrey was suspended from his position on the bench for distributing pornographic and other explicit material from his personal account to

---

[11] http://blogs.wsj.com/law/2014/06/13/judge-rader-author-of-controversial-email -to-lawyer-to-resign-from-bench

others in the state government.[12] A New Mexico judge was forced to resign after admitting that he had sent "excessive and improper" texts to his wife, a court employee, during court proceedings. While he denied that the texts were of a sexual nature, they did include negative remarks about other judges and parties appearing before him.[13] Any neutral who is considering whether to send an email that has potentially offensive content should also consider the impact that its disclosure would have on their career and family. Communicating during a proceeding deprives the parties of the neutral's attention to the case.

Neutrals should also maintain an email address that is separate from their personal email address. If your personal email is breached, having a separate email address will ensure that parties are not contacted, even inadvertently, and it minimizes the likelihood that you might forward that hilarious, yet mildly risqué, joke from your brother-in-law to everyone who appears before you. Personal emails, jokes, and invitations should not be sent to parties appearing before the neutral. Comments on Facebook or blog posts can also compromise the perception of neutrality. A judge in Ottawa retired after crude comments about another judge on Facebook came to light.[14]

Blogs have become less popular with the rise of other social media sites; however, there are still quite a few active blogs, some of which permit comments from other contributors. While reading blogs in your area of law can be a good way to keep abreast of current issues, neutrals should be very hesitant to comment on other people's blog posts. Comments made on a blog or other website can be construed as an opinion or demonstration that your decision-making is influenced by opinions or facts outside of the matters before you. For

---

[12]http://www.philly.com/philly/news/20141021_Supreme_Court_votes_to_su spend_McCaffery_over_e-mails.html

[13] www.kiva.com/news/New-Mexico-judge-resigns-after-allegations-of - sexting-during-court/19210032

[14] http://ottawacitizen.com/news/local-news/ottawa-judge-who-made-crude-facebook-post-retires-rather-than-face-disciplinary-hearing

example, if a neutral were to negatively comment on a blog post about a court decision, the parties who appear before that neutral might believe that the neutral is unable to prevent her personal opinion from affecting their case.

Obviously, the same would be true for a neutral who had their own blog. For that reason, maintaining a personal or professional blog in conjunction with or separate from a professional website should be done with caution. A neutral should never comment on a pending matter or identify parties who appear before them. Additionally, a neutral should never post any materials (e.g., communications or evidence) from a matter that they have heard. Arbitrators should only publish decisions on their personal website if all parties have agreed to their publication. It is appropriate for neutrals who act as fact-finders in the public sector to link to decisions published by a state agency if the neutral is identified in the decision. Likewise, it is appropriate to provide links to decisions published by other legal websites, such as Westlaw or BNA.

Disclosures

What is a friend? What is a colleague? Traditionally, these terms have been fairly obvious, and neutrals have long considered when to disclose these traditional relationships. The rise of social media, however, calls into question the meaning of these terms and how they apply to the increasing number of more tech-savvy neutrals joining the field.

One of the primary ethical duties of every neutral, whether arbitrator, mediator, judge, or fact-finder, is to avoid conflicts of interest and disclose personal relationships with the parties who appear before them. Whether to disclose Facebook "friends" or LinkedIn "connections" is a new consideration for many neutrals.

Social networks create the most significant dilemma for neutrals. It's difficult to avoid the draw of a website on which one can see pictures of one's grandchildren, read articles recommended by smart friends, and get a quick sense of the lives of people one has met and cared for over many years. There is no reason that neutrals should be excluded from these networks. However, internet searching permits parties appearing before a neutral to quickly discover that neutral's "friends," whether or not those connections are relationships that rise to the level of requiring disclosure. Knowing a little about different social networks can help you determine whether you want to be on those networks and how you want to manage your privacy and disclosures about those relationships.

Because Facebook is commonly used as a personal and social networking tool, you should limit your connections on the site to people with whom you've actually socialized, or to whom you are actually connected. That is, Facebook should be used to connect to people who you would already have to disclose if they were a party or witness before you.

If you have connections on Facebook who do not meet that criteria, but who you might still like to connect with in the future for professional reasons, invite them to connect on LinkedIn. Although that might not eliminate the need to disclose the connection in the future, at least it more clearly identifies the nature of your relationship.

> *LinkedIn is a network for maintaining professional connections and can be a great platform for providing potential parties information about your experience and finding groups that may offer robust legal discussions and networking opportunities. Since your connections on LinkedIn might be former or current clients or parties, it is important to disclose your participation in LinkedIn in your disclosure materials. AAA Arbitrator Deborah Masucci suggests using a disclosure similar to the one that she uses:I use a number of online professional networks such as LinkedIn and group email systems. I generally accept requests from other professionals to be added to my LinkedIn website but do not maintain a database of all these professional contacts and connections. LinkedIn now features endorsements, which I do not seek and have no control over who may endorse me for different skills. The existence of such links or endorsements does not indicate any depth or relationship other than*

an online professional connection, similar to connections in professional organizations.[15]

As previously mentioned, there are numerous arbitrators who have not conducted an internet search of their own names. Searching your name and checking the links that appear is important for a number of reasons.

First of all, many parties who consider you for an appointment are going to conduct an internet search before they decide to retain you as a neutral, particularly if they do not have any experience with you in the past. You need to know what they are going to learn when they do. Some parties use services to conduct assessments of neutrals, and others collect information informally from other practitioners. However, most of them are going to conduct a quick internet search, too. The information that they find might not be accurate, current, or useful, but it's what they will rely on to make a decision about you.

Occasionally, the parties will discover something true and relevant about you and your work history or relationships, and which you ought to have disclosed prior to the parties before accepting the appointment. There are at least two California cases where losing parties moved to vacate arbitration awards after finding information about undisclosed relationships that the arbitrator had with one party or their representative. Both involved non-labor cases. They are instructive if you practice in other areas of the law.

In *Mt. Holyoke Homes v. Jeffer Mangels Butler & Mitchell LLP*, (2013) 219 Cal.App.4th 1299, one party discovered, after an internet search, that the arbitrator had listed the other party as a reference on an undisclosed resume that was posted on a website for neutrals.[16] She moved to vacate the arbitration award on the basis that California Code of Civil Procedure §1281.9(a)(6) required disclosure. The Court said:

> *An objective observer reasonably could conclude that an arbitrator listing a prominent litigator as a reference on his resume would be reluctant to rule against the law firm in which that attorney is a partner as a defendant in a legal malpractice action. To entertain a doubt as to whether the arbitrator's interest in maintaining the attorney's high opinion of him could color his judgment in these circumstances is reasonable, is by no means hypersensitive, and requires no reliance on speculation. We believe that an objective observer aware of the facts reasonably could entertain such a doubt.*

More importantly, the Court found that the parties are not obligated to conduct their own research about the arbitrator, noting, "A party to an arbitration is not required to investigate a proposed neutral arbitrator in order to discover information, even public information, that the arbitrator is obligated to disclose. Instead, the obligation rests on the arbitrator to timely make the required disclosure."

In *Casden Park La Brea Retail LLP v. Ross Dress for Less, Inc.* (2008) 162 Cal.App.4th 468, the party seeking to vacate an award similarly conducted an internet search after receiving the award. In that case, the party discovered that the neutral arbitrator on a three-person panel had made campaign contributions to one of the party arbitrators, among other things. The Court of Appeals found that the arbitrator had disclosed prior relationships and had conducted a pre-hearing conference to permit the parties to determine whether they wanted to ask him to withdraw. Although the disclosure had not specifically mentioned the campaign contributions discovered by the moving party, the court declined to uphold the trial court's order to vacate, noting:

> *[Only] significant or substantial business relationships between the neutral arbitrator and a party or his representative must be disclosed to the other party, to avoid the appearance of impropriety, but ordinary and insubstantial business dealings do not necessarily require disclosure...Because arbitrators are selected for their*

familiarity with the type of business dispute involved, they are not expected to be entirely without business contacts in the particular field, but they should disclose any repeated or significant contacts which they may have with a party to the dispute, his attorney or his chosen arbitrator.

Citing Guseinov v. Burns (2006) 145 Cal.App.4th 944, 959.

Ultimately, the modern neutral need not live in a cave, using a typewriter and the post office as their only way to communicate. These basic guidelines will help neutrals access social media in away that avoids landmines such as disclosure and marketing issues.[17]

---

[17] This article was originally published as "Technology and Ethics: A Guide for Neutrals," ABA *Just Resolutions* Newsletter, March 2015. Reprint by permission of the author.

Chapter Six

Publish or Perish

The value of the labor arbitration award was established long before the Supreme Court noted, "A well-reasoned opinion tends to engender confidence in the integrity of the process and aids in clarifying the underlying agreement." *Enterprise Wheel*, 363 US 593 (1960). How then to make well-reasoned opinion known the arbitration audience?

The question of whether to publish arbitration awards arises with some frequency among arbitrators, and you will need to determine whether you'll seek to publish your decisions. In this chapter, I will discuss the arguments for and against publication, provide a brief history of earlier discussions on the topic, and review the current state of labor arbitration publishing. Finally, I will suggest some ideas for a way forward to ensure that new approaches to workplace justice can be shared and discussed.

The Pros and Cons of Publishing

Arbitrators fall into three camps regarding the question of publishing. There are those who regularly submit their awards with the parties' consent. There are others who oppose publishing awards. Finally, there is a much larger group of arbitrators who are either apathetic to the question or find the process of acquiring consent and submitting awards to be a significant hassle that is not worth the time and effort.

I've placed the arguments of the opponents of publication in italics, and address each argument below:

> *Labor arbitration awards are the product of a private contract between private actors and should not be publicized.*

First, I'd like to note that arbitration awards in the public sector do not arise from private contracts. The general public has a right to know how the CBAs in their state or city are interpreted. Other countries require the publication of redacted awards, even in the private sector. Privacy concerns can be addressed through redaction or by publishing summaries. The parties themselves do not keep them confidential. Many party advocates in the private sector routinely share their awards with their peers and with arbitrator evaluation services such as Simpsons.

> *Arbitration awards are so specific to their specific CBA and the facts of the case that they don't offer any general value to the public/reader.*

Obviously, every case depends on the contract language and facts that are specific to that case, but the same is true of legal case decisions that are assumed to be public, unless the parties have requested an order to seal or some other relief from the assumption of non-confidentiality. Court decisions are public because transparency about judicial reasoning is important in a democracy. Public decisions establish norms and increase consistency around legal interpretation. Public decisions answer questions for other cases and interpret the laws in ways that support or curtail others' behavior.

Similarly, the purpose of making awards public is so that the parties, academics, and other arbitrators can consider how arbitrators approach the issues that arise in the unionized workplace. The parties gleam general principles of conflict resolution from awards that are in the public realm.

> *Only arbitrators who are seeking attention submit their decisions.*

Arbitrators who submit awards often do so because it serves as a useful tool for marketing that doesn't run afoul of bar rules on marketing. There are other reasons to publish, however. Some arbitrators want to share their thinking or provide information about a new set of facts or an unusual contractual issue. Arbitrators should publish so that their thinking can be transparent and so that they can contribute to the body of law of the workplace.

> *The publishers only select awards that are unusual and out of line with the thinking of a majority of arbitrators.*

At this point, publishers are likely to publish almost anything that arbitrators submit. As I will discuss below, the current state of available decisions is bleak. If the awards that are published are not very good or are not in keeping with general principles of labor arbitration, it's a "garbage in, garbage out" problem that would be solved by submitting more and better decisions. Arbitrators should forge relationships with publishers to ensure that their editorial oversight is guiding the publication decisions.

> *Published arbitration awards give parties an unrealistic view of how the arbitrator will rule in their case, leading parties to overly rely on existing awards to select arbitrators for their dispute.*

Parties will rely on any information they can find to form opinions about arbitrators. The more an arbitrator publishes, the more parties have to go on. Parties also speak to their colleagues, keep their own records, and use arbitrator evaluations that are either formal or informal. There are often public sector awards, news articles, and other information already available which shape the perception parties have of an arbitrator. As previously mentioned, a remarkable number of arbitrators have never conducted an internet search of their own names. Those who have not researched themselves do not know what the parties are relying on. With publication, you have greater control over the impressions that the parties develop.

> *It's a hassle.*

This is true. It's difficult to ask the parties and often unlikely that both will consent to publication. Tracking who you have asked and who has responded is another administrative task that is cumbersome for those of us who are solo practitioners, as is the submission process to publishers.

How We Got Here

In 1986, Donald Peterson and Julius Rezler, both members of the National Academy of Arbitrators, co-authored a study to understand arbitrators' views of publication and the impact of changes to the NAA Code of Professional Responsibility on arbitrators' willingness to broach the topic with the parties appearing before them.[18] At the NAA Proceedings in the prior years, there was disagreement within the NAA regarding whether and when arbitrators should request to publish their awards; Peterson and Rezler made a valiant effort to support the consensus approach that is reflected in Code of Professional Responsibility 2.C.(c) which states:

It is a violation of professional responsibility for an arbitrator to make public an award without the consent of the parties.

An arbitrator may ask the parties whether they consent to the publication of the award either at the hearing or at the time the award is issued.

(1) If such question is asked at the hearing it should be asked in writing as follows:

"Do you consent to the submission of the award in this matter for publication?

| (…) | (…) |
| YES | NO |

---

[18] The Impact of Opinion 11 on the Publication of Arbitration Awards, JOURNAL OF DISPUTE RESOLUTION, Vol. 1986, Art. 8 (Peterson and Relzig, 1986).

If you consent, you have the right to notify the arbitrator within 30 days after the date of the award that you revoke your consent."

It is desirable but not required that the arbitrator remind the parties at the time of the issuance of the award of their right to withdraw their consent to publication.[19]

The authors favored publication, noting that arbitration awards "facilitate the selection of arbitrators, assist researchers in evaluating trends in arbitration, educate prospective arbitrators, and help the parties in the preparation of their cases and briefs."[20]

The value of publication still exists. In fact, there may be a greater need for access to arbitration awards now than in prior decades. Technology, the internet, COVID-19, legalized drugs, the aging workforce, and cultural changes are all topics for which new ideas and approaches should be shared and vetted in the labor relations community.

Despite the need having grown, the avenues for publication have narrowed. The Bureau of National Affairs (BNA) was purchased by Bloomberg in 2011, which stopped publishing hard copies of BNA Labor Reports in 2019. Labor Reports are available from Bloomberg Law, but only with a subscription to the entire Bloomberg Law database. The estimated cost for a solo provider subscription is more than $7,000 per year. Thomson Reuters bought Westlaw in 2010 and CCH in 2012. An all-inclusive Thomson Reuters subscription for a solo practitioner is approximately $240 per month (i.e., $2,880 per year). Thomson Reuters does not publish physical arbitration awards either.

The end of paper publications, along with the high cost associated with accessing online databases, are not the only barriers for arbitrators, researchers, and parties to learn more about current labor arbitration issues. A bigger hurdle is the willingness of parties to agree to publication and of arbitrators to submit their awards. Without content to publish, it doesn't matter what the publishers charge.

---

[19] https://naarb.org/code-of-professional-responsibility/
[20] Peterson and Relzig, p. 1.

Without current arbitration awards available to labor relations specialists, arbitral jurisprudence cannot evolve. Likewise, arbitrators and parties cannot review traditional labor principles to test their applicability to the modern workplace. Unions, employers, and arbitrators cannot revise cultural standards in the workplace, such as those governing harassment, workplace violence, or implicit bias.

Remedies

There are several remedies for this information gap, some of which are easier to implement than others:

Arbitrators should make a greater effort to get parties to agree to publication, such as offering to submit redacted awards to reduce the parties' concerns about sharing their losses.

Request for publication can be made after the issuance of the award so that the parties do not feel pressure to agree as a condition of receiving the award. Submitting requests for publication once per year (e.g., at the end of the year) focuses the administrative task and distinguishes the request for publication from the issuance of the award. I try to do this at the end of each year. Below, this is the language that I sent at the end of 2020:

I hope this email finds you well and enjoying a restful holiday season.

> *I am reviewing my files to determine whether any of my 2021 decisions are appropriate to submit for publication to BNA. At the time, I issued the enclosed award, I notified you an arbitrator may not ethically offer an opinion for publication without the consent of the parties and requested that you let me know if you objected to the publication of this award. I have decided to offer the opinion for publication with all witness and grievant names redacted. Please let me know if you object to me doing so. If I do not hear from you by January 14, 2021, I will submit them to BNA for consideration. If you let me know after that date, I will of course inform the publisher.*

Thank you very much for your consideration. Have a very happy New Year.

Other remedies are out of arbitrators' hands. Public sector arbitration awards should be public records. In some states, interest arbitration awards and, less frequently, grievance arbitration decisions are published on state websites. In other cases, they are considered public records subject to state and federal sunshine laws. States and municipalities should consider legislation requiring that redacted decisions in the public sector be available to the public.

Parties should permit the publication of partially redacted or unredacted decisions regardless of the outcome. The labor and employment bar should consider undertaking a discussion among practitioners regarding the value of supporting publication, particularly if awards can be redacted in a way that removes any personally identifying information about grievants and witnesses from being disclosed.

Non-profit and educational institutions should find ways to make labor arbitration decisions accessible at a low cost. The National Academy of Arbitrators could collaborate with public institutions to promote publication in a public format so that the cost barriers are not as cumbersome for researchers and the general public.

The Code of Professional Responsibility could be amended to allow arbitrators to submit fully redacted decisions without the parties' consent. This is the most controversial idea. However, redacted or summarized awards would help arbitrators, researchers, advocates, and the general public better understand labor law, industrial justice, and labor arbitration.

Obviously, some of these suggestions are more controversial than others, while some are more difficult to implement. What is evident, however, is that the labor relations community requires more arbitration awards about more topics on more platforms that are available at a lower cost. As an arbitrator, determine how you can increase the level of transparency in decision-making.

Chapter Seven

Lessons From the Pandemic

When the federal and state governments began to impose quarantines amidst the rising number of COVID-19-related deaths, arbitrators and neutrals rolled with the prevailing view that our cases would be delayed for a short time. However, as hearing cancellations began to mount, we wondered whether this was an opportunity to develop our skills at remote hearings.

Not every arbitrator took advantage of the crisis to expand their skills, of course. Some retired, while others continued in-person hearings to the extent that they were permitted or welcomed by the parties. Notably, early in the pandemic, the National Academy of Arbitrators (NAA) recognized that a formal approach to remote hearings would be needed to ensure consistency, integrity, and trust in the arbitration process. The Videoconference Task Force was established, and in April 2020, began offering training for arbitrators and advocates on how to conduct remote hearings.[21] The Task Force offered ongoing training and conducted regular office hours to help practitioners and arbitrators troubleshoot both technical and ethical issues as they arose.

From the outset, the NAA and individual arbitrators created video hearing procedures to educate advocates regarding the process of conducting remote hearings.[22] As the procedures have evolved,

---

[21] https://naarb.org/videoconferencing/

[22] https://naarb.org/wp-content/uploads/2020/03/VideoconferencingProcedures.pdf

many labor arbitrators have come to see remote hearings as an opportunity to expand access to workplace justice for unionized workers, their unions, and their employers.

Most of the changes to labor arbitration as a result of the pandemic have been positive, yet some changes have demonstrated the limitations of video hearings. Nevertheless, labor arbitration and adjudicatory procedures are being transformed; technologies and procedures have changed, the nature of the cases we hear has changed, and the people who are able to participate have changed. I will touch on each area below, although many changes have overlapping impacts. These changes raise opportunities for affordability, efficiency, and inclusivity.

Technology

The first and most obvious change has been the adoption of different video platforms to host hearings. Often, the platform is selected by the party who is willing to host, and that is usually the arbitrator or someone who hosts on their behalf, such as a court reporting service or a technician hired for that purpose. People are able to use personal computers, laptops, cell phones, or tablets to participate, although internet access can be the wild card, even for neutrals.

Some parties fear that internet access will prevent working people from participating in video forums. However, 93% of Americans use the internet, including 96% of people aged 50-64, 98% of people aged 30-49, and 99% of people aged 18-29.[23] That includes 91% of African-Americans and 95% of Hispanic Americans. Additionally, 91% of Americans making $30,000-$49,999 use the internet, and 98% of those making $50,000-$74,999 do as well. The pandemic likely accelerated the trend. The number of people who have home broadband increased to 77% by February 2021.[24] Thus, it seems

---

[23] https://www.pewresearch.org/internet/fact-sheet/internet-broadband/#smartphone-dependency-over-time
[24] Id.

unlikely that internet access persists as a barrier to participation by working-class employees.

In fact, remote hearings have increased access for union members who want to watch proceedings or participate from their worksites when they might otherwise have been unable to do so. It became the norm for witnesses to appear via video conference from their cars, homes, and workplace break rooms. As a result, they did not have to miss work, travel, or decline to participate due to the difficulty of appearing in person.

Overall, remote hearings are less resource-intensive and, thus, less costly. The cost of the video platform is borne at a small cost by the host, usually the arbitrator, and spread across dozens of cases in a year. In-person hearings require space, travel expenses, lost time, and associated costs, such as refreshments and audiovisual assistance. Remote hearings save parties the arbitrator's travel time and expense, as well as any costs associated with having attorneys and witnesses travel to a hearing.

The ability to share documents electronically, now customary in video hearings, also means that less paper is used. Minimizing air travel not only saves money, but also reduces the carbon emissions associated with travel. Remote hearings are better for the environment than in-person hearings.

The use of a court reporter's service is sometimes contentious, particularly when one party wishes to spare the expense and the other believes that it is necessary to create a record. Remote hearings can alleviate the need for a court reporter if the arbitrator and parties agree that the hearing can be recorded on the video platform. However, some arbitrators may hesitate to allow video because of their concerns about security and privacy and the later use and misuse of the footage. Other arbitrators prefer the assistance of the court reporter in conducting the hearing and prefer a transcript as the official record of the hearing. Finally, the arbitrator should be clear about what constitutes the official record of the proceedings and the disposition of the video.

Procedures

As noted above, many arbitrators created new procedures to increase the parties' comfort and familiarity with remote hearings. Some of these new procedures resulted in better and more streamlined hearings from the perspective of the neutral.

At first, more arbitrators adopted pre-hearing conferences in order to teach the participants how to use the video platform technology, but quickly realized that these pre-hearing conferences allowed them to learn about the issues in the case, answer questions about subpoenas and documentary evidence, determine the time needed to complete the hearing, and schedule the hearing and briefing. These pre-hearing conferences encouraged the parties to acquaint themselves with their own cases and resulted in more stipulations, joint exhibits and statements of the issue, and settlements prior to the hearing.

Parties needed to identify witnesses and documents earlier in the hearing process, which resulted in counsel being better prepared for the hearing and to present their case in a more professional and efficient manner. Some attorneys argue that they miss the ability to provide dramatic or antagonistic effects to their arguments. However, arbitrators view pugnacious presentations as a show for the client, not the arbitrator, and the absence of histrionics improves the quality of the overall record when it comes time to decide the case.

Another innovation of the remote hearing process was a change to standard witness admonitions. Whereas witnesses are sworn in at in-person hearings and told to speak up for the court reporter, I added a series of additional questions:

1. Are you alone in the room where you are currently located? (For reference, moral support for the grievant is permitted, as well as children in the witness's care.)
2. Do you have any documents other than exhibits provided by the representative? Please be aware that if you refer to another document off-camera, it will need to be introduced into evidence.

3. Do understand that you cannot record any part of this proceeding for your use or distribution? The arbitrator is solely responsible for the official record in this case.

4. Please turn off any personal devices you have and move them out of reach so that you are not distracted or tempted to communicate with anyone while you are testifying.

There have been several cases reported in legal publications about witnesses who were being coached by someone off-camera or via text message; however, those are likely a rare exception. In labor arbitration, at least, we have to trust the parties and witnesses that the integrity of the process is valuable to their ongoing labor relations and that trickery will be discovered. Witnesses can be kept in the "main room" of a video hearing while the parties confer in breakout rooms and should be reminded not to contact or communicate with counsel or the parties during breaks in their testimony.

Another advantage to remote hearings is the ability of the arbitrator to better control the proceedings by using the tools within the video platform. For example, witnesses can be kept in the "waiting room." Parties can be provided with breakout rooms for caucuses and breaks, and the breakout rooms can be closed by the arbitrator to ensure that the parties return to the hearing in a timely fashion, which isn't something we've figured out how to do in person. Arbitrators can even mute individuals who are interrupting others or being excessively argumentative or difficult. I only had to do that once in a remote hearing, but it was more effective than "taking counsel out into the hallway" to admonish them.

Participants

Video hearings have expanded the number of people who can participate in hearings. First, the parties have a wider field of arbitrators from which to choose because they do not need to pay travel fees to engage an arbitrator from outside their immediate area. This is particularly valuable for cases in locations where there are very few arbitrators, such as rural locations and far-flung cities such as Fairbanks, Alaska. Having a large pool of arbitrators from which to choose means that it can be easier to schedule a hearing date.

The number of witnesses who can participate has also expanded. In the past, it was difficult to secure the release of multiple employees for a hearing. As noted above, the availability of cell phones and broadband across the spectrum of possible witnesses means that people can appear for a brief time without traveling, missing work, or being present for far longer than necessary to share their testimony. Witnesses are also more comfortable testifying from a familiar location such as their home, car, or break room, and do not become overwhelmed by the unfamiliar and legalistic setting used for hearings.

Finally, more observers can be accommodated in video hearings. Again, unions and employers might previously have hesitated to include others who needed training in the grievance and arbitration process because of the lost time and expense of including them. However, many hearings now include new HR staff, stewards, and counsel who are observing in order to learn about the process. Union members who want to observe are able to do so for however long makes sense for them, instead of needing to change their work schedule to participate.

Some parties who would otherwise use a court reporter might no longer believe that they need to if the arbitrator is willing to record the proceedings. In cases where the parties still want a court reporter, video hearings are preferable to in-person hearings when masking is common. Court reporters are much better able to transcribe the proceedings via video conference than they are in person. Masked witnesses can be difficult to hear, and many court reporters rely on lip reading to assist them. Masks make that impossible.

Cases

Because of early quarantine measures, most people adapted to doing all kinds of cases in the form of remote hearings. There were several industries that insisted on in-person hearings (e.g., law enforcement), but that resulted in major delays to those cases, which could not be held due to state and local prohibitions on meetings. Other industries found that remote hearings were preferable to in-person hearings, and certain kinds of cases are more suitable for remote hearings than others. Parties who have expedited hearings appreciate being able to have multiple cases heard on the same day. Additionally, cases that have many stipulated facts and documents are also well-suited for remote hearing.

In industries where management leaders, legal counsel, and frontline staff are not located in the same vicinity, video hearings made scheduling the necessary participants much easier and less expensive. This is the case, for example, in the railroad and airline industries. I suspect that video hearings will become permanent in many contracts and administrative hearings as parties look for ways to increase efficiency and decrease costs.

Common Concerns

As parties have struggled to "re-open" and "get back to normal" despite ongoing COVID-19 concerns, several have raised issues to arbitrators regarding the use of video hearings. One common concern is that arbitrators are not able to judge the credibility of their witnesses because they are less able to observe body language. However, very few arbitrators rely on "demeanor" to judge credibility. Doing so introduces a degree of bias that should be acknowledged and eliminated. For example, many people are nervous about being in a legal proceeding for personal and cultural reasons. The fact that they may fidget, appear anxious, or struggle to testify should not be taken as a sign of lesser credibility. Arbitrators rely on testimonial evidence, not perceptions of truthfulness in body language. In fact, being able to look directly at the witness's face while they testify from a comfortable location makes it easier to understand their testimony and judge its factual value.

Some people are concerned that witnesses may not have access to dependable wireless or broadband to appear by video, and, in particular, believe that an equity issue might arise if working-class employees are required to have internet access that isn't provided by the employer. First of all, as the aforementioned Pew Research statistics indicate, people from a broad spectrum of American society have access to the internet. Second, it is the responsibility of the party calling the witness to provide access to reliable internet service to ensure that they can testify. Finally, if all else fails, just as the internet often does, people can appear by telephone to provide their testimony. This was an available solution before the pandemic, which was largely unquestioned.

Some arbitrators say that they prefer in-person hearings because they like to be around other people. Many arbitrators work alone and like the opportunity to connect in person. However, just as many arbitrators prefer remote hearing for the safety it affords them. With an average age above 65, many labor arbitrators are in a commonly accepted risk group, particularly those who also have chronic conditions that they might rather not share with the parties. Workplace safety extends to the hearing for witnesses, counsel, and the arbitrator, and video hearings increase that safety.

There are, of course, ergonomic issues that arise when we are staring at a screen for hours at a time. The arbitrator needs to build in regular breaks, just as they would in an in-person hearing.

Although many of the common concerns have reasonable answers, video hearings are not great for every forum. By necessity, parties have conducted contract negotiations by video conference, and it will be interesting to see whether that persists. Mediation can be more difficult via video and is still adapting to the format. In mediation, the parties and mediator rely on tension, timing, and body language to convey information that may not translate to a small screen. In person, it can be effective to hold recalcitrant parties in the room together to keep them engaged and moving forward. When someone can move around their house in a distracted fashion or even leave a video hearing with the touch of a button, it's very hard to reach a settlement.

On balance, many neutrals have embraced video hearings and will probably look for new ways to innovate the practice so that parties can have their grievances heard in a timely and efficient manner without losing the human contact that makes labor law so compelling.[25]

---

[25] This article was originally prepared for the Union Lawyers Alliance Conference in May 2022. I appeared remotely on a panel about the impact of the pandemic on hearings because I had recently tested positive for COVID-19.

Chapter Eight

Ending an Arbitration Practice

I assume that very few experienced arbitrators are looking to me for advice on closing their practice. However, even newer arbitrators should be planning for the end, even if it's twenty years away. Planning ahead will make it easier to focus on the present. The reality of our profession is that not everyone has a successful arbitration practice, and planning will help you decide if it's time to try something different in your career.

For some arbitrators, ending their practice is as simple as sending out letters to all of their panels and appointing agencies, writing their final awards, and scheduling a tee time. Other arbitrators leave their practice feet first, with hearings on the calendar and unwritten decisions in the queue. Whether you hope to retire and travel the world or want to stick with your practice until they pry a transcript from your hands, you should plan for both possible outcomes.

Line Up the Experts

Hopefully, you have not waited until you've been in practice for 25 years to consult a financial planner and estate planner. I am sure that I sound like a broken record but whether you have do so yet or not, it is imperative that you meet with your planners at least every five years, if not more often. It's important that they know what your preference is for managing the end of your career. In addition to your wills and trusts, these experts can help you keep tabs on your retirement and when you must draw pensions and social security; understand the tax implications of continuing to work; and offer advice regarding ending a business or law practice in your state.

Develop Your Bench or Form a Tag Team

If something happens to you, whether short-term or permanent in nature, that prevents you from working, someone will need to communicate with parties and agencies on your behalf. You may need someone to help finish writing some decisions or finding out party preferences for moving forward. If there is a rising arbitrator you mentor, it may make sense to identify that person and let them know who can help them access your files, such as your spouse or your assistant. Another option is to form a "tag team" with another arbitrator who will assist if something goes wrong and who you will assist if an emergency arises in their practice.

In some cases, NAA Regional groups can help identify arbitrators who can assist on short notice. For example, I know one arbitrator who retired relatively early and has assisted in winding down the practice of a few arbitrators who died unexpectedly. Make sure that your passwords and contacts are accessible to at least one person (e.g., a spouse or offspring) who will be able to assist.

Refresh Your Contacts

If your next-of-kin needed to get in touch with everyone who needed to know that you are no longer practicing, would they be able to find that information? In most cases, the answer is no. Very few of us keep a paper address book that identifies our contacts. You don't need to tackle your whole contact list at once, but as you close cases, update the contacts in your email program and note the date that you made any changes. Be sure that your next-of-kin is aware that they should notify FMCS, AAA, your state appointing agencies, and the National Academy of Arbitrators. These organizations can assist in getting the word out, if necessary.

Plan Your Schedule Ahead

This may seem like common sense, but if you want to slow down, you need to schedule fewer cases. Many established arbitrators set cases up to a year in advance, making it very difficult to pivot to a lower caseload. Look out past your last hearing date and start blocking off weeks now. Schedule that time for yourself or your family and treat it like a real appointment. If you want to go half-time, block off half the time, and so forth. Let people know that you are reducing your caseload, retiring, or narrowing the focus of your practice, at least one year ahead of time. It takes at least that long for them to believe it's true.

Tell Your Partner!

This is another obvious point, but keeping all of this information in one handy place that your spouse or next-of-kin knows about is absolutely necessary. They'll need passwords, contacts, account numbers, insurance information, office keys, names of your accountant and lawyer, the name of your successor arbitrator, and mailbox information. They'll have to figure out who will be the executor of your firm, and you should have written instructions regarding what you want to happen.

Know When to Fold 'Em

As I write this, my state is represented by an octogenarian in the United States Senate. This is a matter of great consternation to me because I don't believe that this senator has a grasp of the seriousness of the issues facing our country or the mental acuity to do anything about them. I happen to live in California, but I suspect that are quite a few senators who match this description. It makes me wonder how I will know when it's time to retire.

I was once privy to a conversation—actually more of an intervention—among more experienced arbitrators who were telling one of their colleagues that it was time to retire. He was having a difficult time finishing decisions, his wife feared for his safety driving long distances, and his reputation was beginning to sour among the parties who had once eagerly selected him. Due to his longstanding reputation, he still received work, but his wife's concerns spurred his colleagues to have a very difficult conversation with him at a conference we all attended. I was mortified to watch it. Maybe it will occur to me one day that I'd rather be doing something else, but what if that day never comes? I don't want a posse of my colleagues to corner me and tell me to retire.

The solution, if there is one, is to be ready to retire on short notice if circumstances warrant it, and to set a deadline or benchmarks earlier in your career that you can refer to as the time comes. Maybe I will review my career at 70, or perhaps I will wait until my grandchildren are walking. Maybe I'll say that I'll retire after my one-thousandth case, or even my three-thousandth case. Nevertheless, I hope that I have the good sense to leave on the early side. After all, I want to preserve my integrity and enjoy the fruits of my labor. As they say in show business, I want to "leave them wanting more."

Acknowledgements

I want to thank the many arbitrators and practitioners who have provided me with valuable support and wisdom over the past few years, both in my practice and in the preparation of this book. Dan Altemus, Tom Angelo, Bonnie Bogue, Margie Brogan, Barbra Chvaney, Brian Clauss, Judy Coffin, Buddy Cohn, Jerilou Cossack, Peter Dahlens, Barbara Diamond, Fred D'Orazio, Rafael Gely, Kristina Hillman, Frederick Horwitz, Anita Christine Knowlton, Darren Lee, Toni Littlestone, Marty Malin, Anita Martinez, Gerald McKay, Paul Roose, Frank Silver, Cheryl Stevens, David Weinberg, and Barry Winograd. I especially want to thank Brook Dooley and our sons Liam and Quinn for their love and curiosity about this mysterious job that I have.

www.ingramcontent.com/pod-product-compliance
Lightning Source LLC
Chambersburg PA
CBHW071118210326
41519CB00020B/6334